Coding
Onstage

By Colleen van Lent and Kristin Fontichiaro

Published in the United States of America by Cherry Lake Publishing
Ann Arbor, Michigan
www.cherrylakepublishing.com

Series Adviser: Kristin Fontichiaro
Reading Adviser: Marla Conn, MS, Ed., Literacy specialist, Read-Ability, Inc.

Image Credits: Various images throughout courtesy of Scratch

Library of Congress Cataloging-in-Publication Data

Names: van Lent, Colleen, author. | Fontichiaro, Kristin, author.
Title: Coding onstage / by Colleen van Lent and Kristin Fontichiaro.
Description: Ann Arbor, Michigan : Cherry Lake Publishing, 2020. | Series: Operation code | Includes bibliographical references and index. |
    Audience: Grades 2-3
Identifiers: LCCN 2019035873 (print) | LCCN 2019035874 (ebook) | ISBN 9781534159280 (hardcover) | ISBN 9781534161580 (paperback) |
    ISBN 9781534160439 (pdf) | ISBN 9781534162730 (ebook)
Subjects: LCSH: Computer programming—Juvenile literature. | Scratch (Computer program language)—Juvenile literature.
Classification: LCC QA76.6115 .V36 2020 (print) | LCC QA76.6115 (ebook) | DDC 005.13/3–dc23
LC record available at https://lccn.loc.gov/2019035873
LC ebook record available at https://lccn.loc.gov/2019035874

Cherry Lake Publishing would like to acknowledge the work of the Partnership for 21st Century Learning, a Network of Battelle for Kids.
Please visit *http://www.battelleforkids.org/networks/p21* for more information.

Printed in the United States of America
Corporate Graphics

NOTE TO READERS: Use this book to practice your Scratch 3 coding skills. If you have never used Scratch before, ask a parent, teacher, or librarian to help you set up an account at *https://scratch.mit.edu*. Read the tutorials on the website to learn how Scratch works. Then you will be ready for the activities in this book! You will practice using variables, if/then statements, copying code to other sprites, using effects to change a sprite's look, and more! Find all the starter and final programs at *https://scratch.mit.edu/users/CherryLakeCoding*.

Table of Contents

Let's Dance! 5

Starting Positions 7

Gloria, the Gliding Dancer 9

Jade, the Jumping Dancer 11

Repeating Jumps 13

Changing Jade's Costumes 15

Nia, the Prima Ballerina 17

Adding Music 19

Your Next Performance 21

Glossary 22

Find Out More 23

Index 24

About the Authors 24

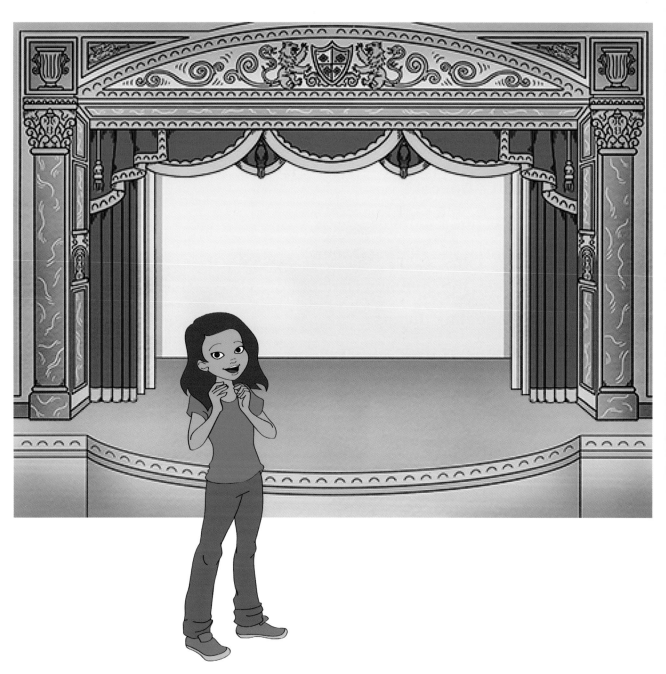

Let's Dance!

I'm Abby. I am the **choreographer** for the fall ballet. Help me code new **choreography**!

I got things started at *https://scratch.mit. edu/projects/309239471*. Can you help me with the rest?

Pro Tip!
Scratch lets you see other people's projects and copy them to make them your own. My code contains the **sprites**, backdrops, and music choices we will use in this book.

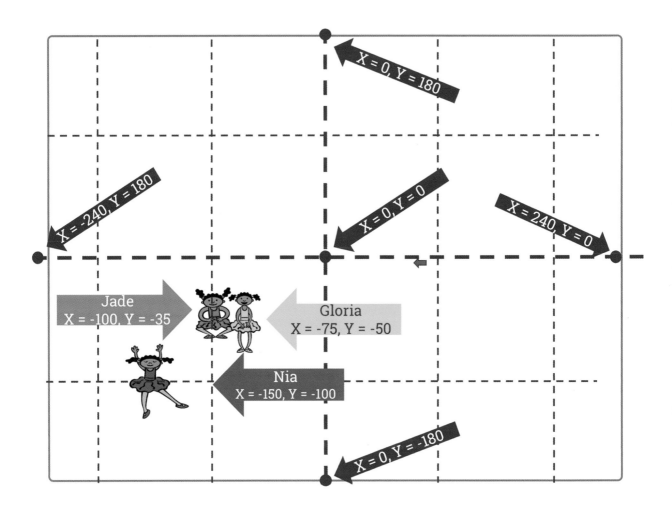

Starting Positions

Scratch uses a grid and numbers called **coordinates** to place the **ballerinas**. The x-coordinate tells how far left or right they should be. The y-coordinate tells how far up or down they are.

I already placed each ballerina onstage at her starting point.

Pro Tip!

Each ballerina needs her own code to know where to go. Click on a sprite to edit her code.

Beginning of
the program ·················○

Gloria starts at
this location ·················○

Moves Gloria ·················○
to the right

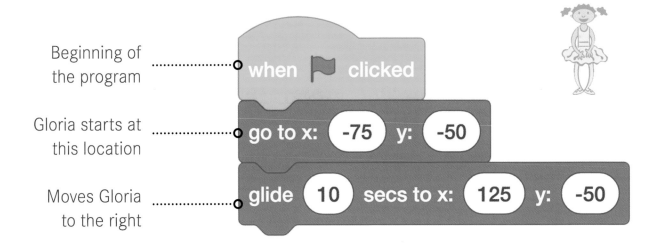

when 🚩 clicked

go to x: -75 y: -50

glide 10 secs to x: 125 y: -50

Gloria, the Gliding Dancer

Click on Gloria. Her choreography is to glide across the stage. Add the `glide ( ) secs to x: ( ) y: ( )` Motion block to the code.

Change the numbers in the `glide ( ) secs to x: ( ) y: ( )` block to match the one here. The first number is how many seconds it takes Gloria to move. The x- and y-coordinate numbers are her final position.

Pro Tip!

Don't use Motion blocks like `move ( ) steps` and `go to x: ( ) y: ( )`. These blocks move Gloria too fast.

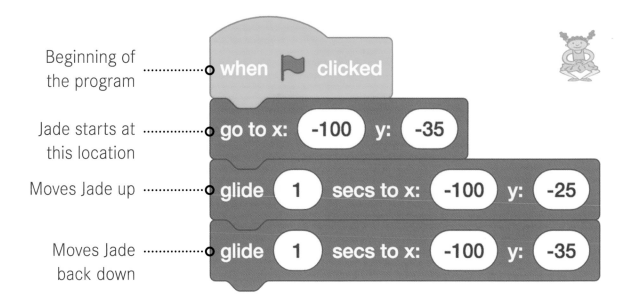

Beginning of the program ⋯⋯⋯⋯⋯o when ⚑ clicked

Jade starts at this location ⋯⋯⋯⋯o go to x: -100 y: -35

Moves Jade up ⋯⋯⋯⋯o glide 1 secs to x: -100 y: -25

Moves Jade back down ⋯⋯⋯⋯o glide 1 secs to x: -100 y: -35

Jade, the Jumping Dancer

Click on Jade. Her choreography is jumping. The y-coordinate will change, but the x-coordinate will stay the same.

You need to add two `glide ( ) secs to x: ( ) y: ( )` Motion blocks: one to go up and one to come down. Add the coordinates shown here. Then click `when ⚑ clicked` to see what happens.

Pro Tip!

Look at the area below the stage. Watch Jade's coordinates change as she moves. Did you notice that only the y changed? That is because she only moved up and down.

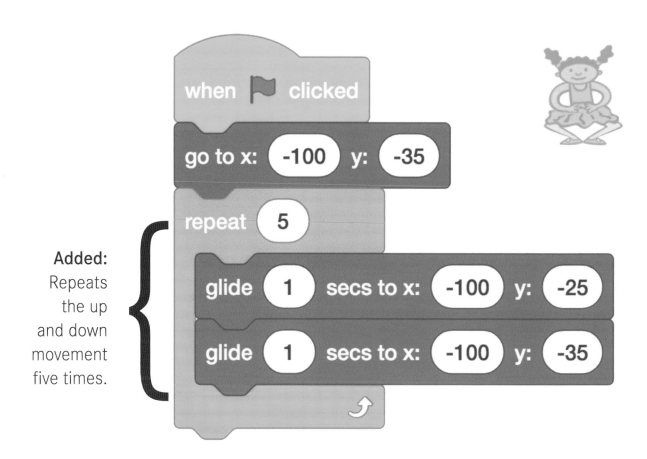

Added:
Repeats
the up
and down
movement
five times.

Repeating Jumps

One jump isn't enough. How about five jumps? We could copy our code five times. Or we can use this Control block:

Drag this block glide ⬤ secs to x: ⬤ y: ⬤ above the two Motion blocks you want to repeat. It will wrap around both blocks. Don't forget to update the number in your Control block!

Pro Tip!

Did your *repeat* Control block not go where you wanted? Sometimes it takes a few tries to get your code working just right. Try inserting it right above the first *glide* Motion block.

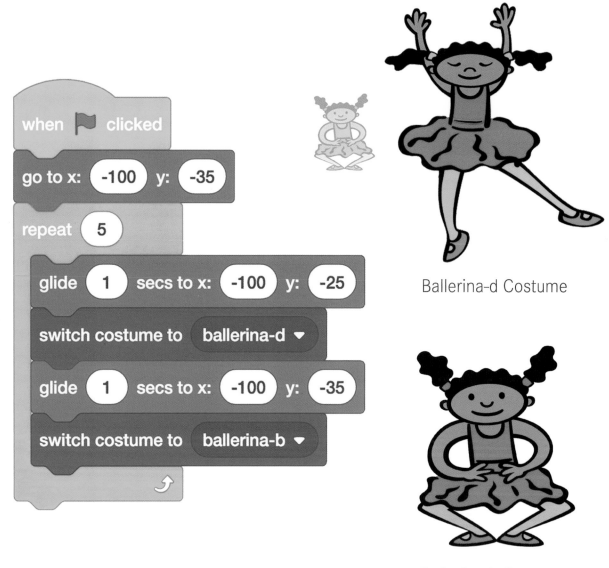

when ⚑ clicked

go to x: -100 y: -35

repeat 5

  glide 1 secs to x: -100 y: -25

  switch costume to ballerina-d ▾

  glide 1 secs to x: -100 y: -35

  switch costume to ballerina-b ▾

Ballerina-d Costume

Ballerina-b Costume

Changing Jade's Costumes

Jade has four different positions. Scratch calls positions costumes. Let's change Jade's costume so she leaps when she is up.

Add two `switch costume to ◯` Looks blocks to Jade's code. Make sure to select which costumes you want to switch between. Then test it out at least twice.

Pro Tip!

You can also use the Costumes tab to change a sprite. Gloria, Jade, and Nia all started as the same sprite. We used the Costumes tab to change the color of their **tutus** so they looked different.

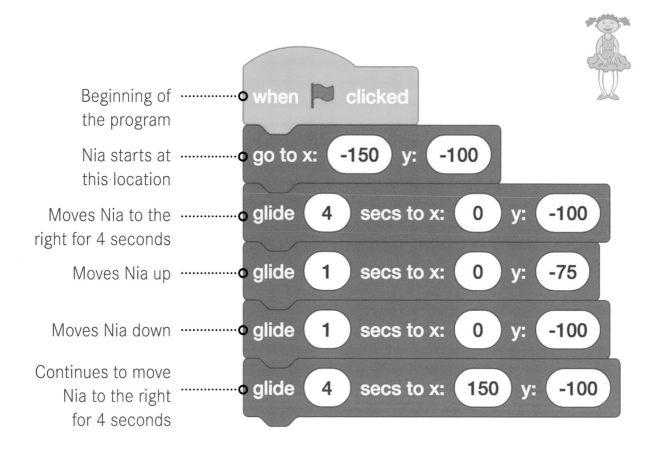

Beginning of the program .... when 🏴 clicked

Nia starts at this location .... go to x: -150 y: -100

Moves Nia to the right for 4 seconds .... glide 4 secs to x: 0 y: -100

Moves Nia up .... glide 1 secs to x: 0 y: -75

Moves Nia down .... glide 1 secs to x: 0 y: -100

Continues to move Nia to the right for 4 seconds .... glide 4 secs to x: 150 y: -100

Nia, the Prima Ballerina

Click on Nia, the **prima ballerina**. She can glide side to side *and* jump up and down. Let's help her do both.

Change her x- or y-coordinates. Check out our code to see what we did. Change the code to choreograph your own one-of-a-kind dance!

Pro Tip!

Don't waste time trying to guess the correct x- and y-coordinates! Instead, move the sprite with your mouse. Scratch will show you the x- and y-coordinates in the list of blocks.

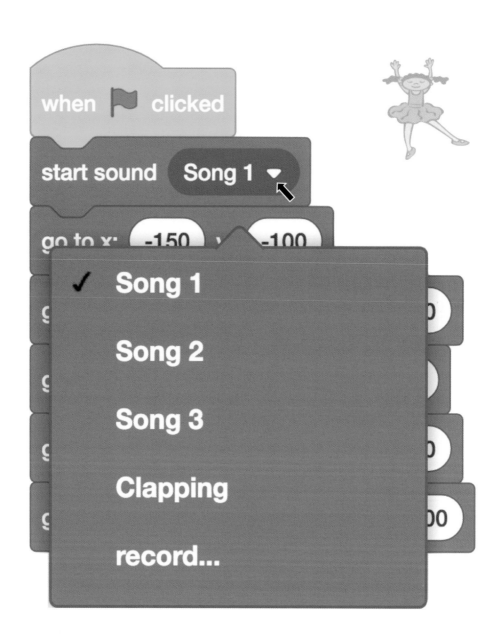

Adding Music

Music helps dancers know when they should move. Let's add a start sound  Sound block to Nia's code. Drag the block underneath the when ⚑ clicked Events block.

Click the arrow on the start sound block to pick a song.

Pro Tip!

Want to change to a new sound? Click the Sounds tab (next to Costumes) at the top of your screen. You can even make sounds go slower or faster!

Your Next Performance

Can you add more to your ballet?

Here are a few ideas:

- Add another dancer.
- Change the costume of one of the dancers.
- Change the tutu colors.
- Add snowflakes for **scenery**.

What other ideas do you have?

Pro Tip!

If you would like to see our final code, go to
https://scratch.mit.edu/projects/309235132.

Glossary

ballerinas (bal-uh-REE-nuhz) female ballet dancers

choreographer (kor-ee-AH-gruh-fur) someone who decides how dancers should move onstage

choreography (kor-ee-AH-gruh-fee) dance moves

coordinates (koh-OR-duh-nits) numbers that tell you the location of a sprite

prima ballerina (PREE-muh ball-uh-REE-nuh) term used to describe the best female dancer

scenery (SEE-nur-ee) features that set the scene of a play or other presentation

sprites (SPRYTS) characters or objects in Scratch

tutus (TOO-tooz) short, fluffy skirts worn by ballerinas

Find Out More

Books

LEAD Project. *Super Scratch Programming Adventure!*
   San Francisco, California: No Starch Press, 2019.

Lovett, Amber. *Coding with Blockly.* Ann Arbor, Michiganl:
   Cherry Lake Publishing, 2017.

Websites

Scratch
http://scratch.mit.edu
Build your Scratch code online at this site.

Scratch Wiki
https://en.scratch-wiki.info
If you get stuck, ask an adult to help you look on this site for advice.

Index

backdrops, 5
ballerinas, 7

choreography, 5, 9, 11
color, 15
Control block, 13, 18–19
coordinates, 7
costumes, 14–15

down movement, 11

Events block, 19

glide Motion block, 8, 9, 10, 13, 16–17
go to x Motion blocks, 8, 9, 10

jump Motion block, 11, 17

leaping, 15
Looks block, 15

Motion block, 9, 11, 13, 17
move x steps Motion block, 9
music, 5, 18–19

positions, 15

repeat Control block, 12, 13

Sound block, 18–19
sprites, 5, 15
start sound Sound block, 19
switch costume Looks block, 14–15

testing, 15

up movement, 11

x-coordinate, 7, 9, 11, 17

y-coordinate, 7, 9, 11, 17

About the Authors

Colleen van Lent teaches coding and Web design at the University of Michigan School of Information. She has three cool kids and a dog named Bacon. She wishes she could touch her toes.

Kristin Fontichiaro teaches at the University of Michigan School of Information. She likes working with kids on creative projects from coding to sewing to junk box inventions. She has written or edited almost 100 books for kids.